FAMILY TIMELINE

Model T Ford

World War I 1914-18

First Radio Broadcast

The Great Depression

Lindberg's Flight

World War II 1939-45

1907	1908	1914	1918	1920	1927	1929	1930	1931	1937	1939	1944	1945	1947	1949

- 1907 — John H. Yoder Died
- 1908 — Fanny Yoder Born
- 1918 — Edna Hochstetler's Car Accident
- 1927 — Abe Stoll & Fanny Yoder Married
- 1929 — Iva Stoll Born
- 1931 — Twila Stoll Born
- 1937 — Joyce Stoll Born
- 1939 — Ardys Stoll Born
- 1944 — Stoll Family Moved To Casselton
- 1945 — Rhoda Yoder Died
- 1947 — Terry Stoll Born
- 1949 — John Stoll Born

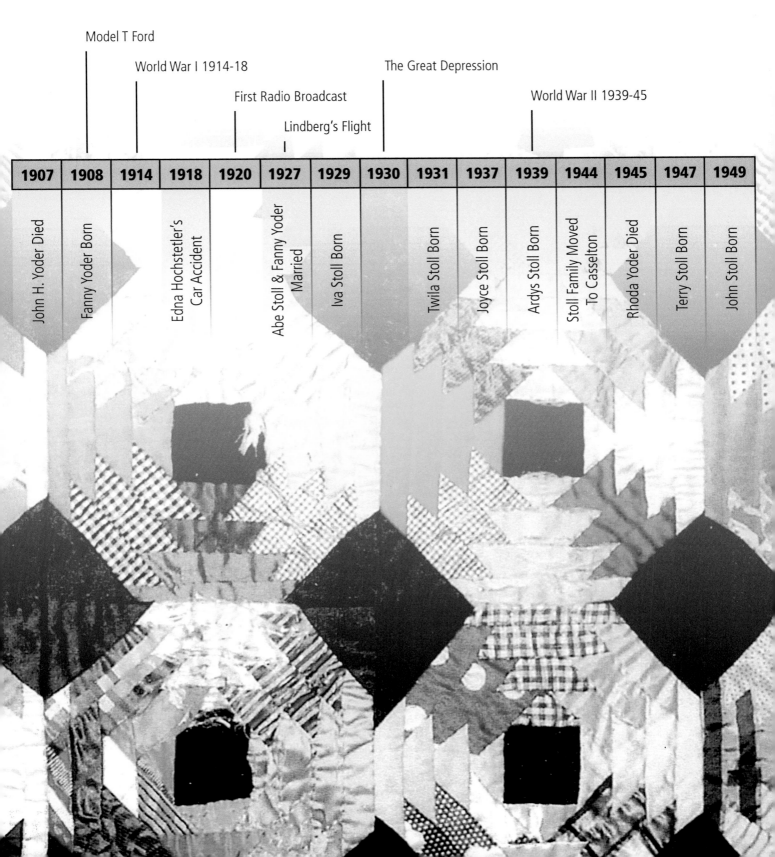

The Twice Said Farm

a memoir of grandma rhoda

BY TWILA SCHROCK

The Twice Paid Farm — A Memoir of Grandma Rhoda

Copyright © 2011 by Twila Schrock

Second Printing 2020

Cover and Text Design by Jim L. Friesen

Library of Congress Control Number: 2011905615

International Standard Book Number: 978-0-9834062-4-2

Printed in the United States of America by Mennonite Press, Inc., Newton, KS, www.mennonitepress.com

dedicated to

Rhoda Yoder's descendants

a special thanks to

Laurie Robinson, *writing coach*

Melanie Zuercher, *editor*

Joan Schrock Woodward, *editor*

Members of my immediate and extended family,
for their input and genealogical information

Supportive friends and neighbors

Kauffman Museum, North Newton, KS

prologue

There are many family stories about my grandma Rhoda Yoder, a pioneer on the Midwest prairies, passed down to me, one of her granddaughters. Rhoda's homestead farm was located on the top of a rising hill where she could see for miles around. No trees or buildings obstructed the view—there was only a huge inverted bowl of deep blue sky over the grassy prairies.

My Grandma Rhoda, a 33-year-old widow, along with her mother, Elizabeth Kauffman, smoked corncob pipes while sitting around an open fire with Chippewa Indians in the vast prairies of North Dakota. They had no common language—only with gestures, grunts, many smiles, pointing motions and other sign language, and puffs on their pipes did they communicate enough to make a trade. (One time Rhoda traded a ham for 20 gallons of juneberries.)

Imagine the contrasts: leather moccasins next to black, high-top, button shoes; unwashed leather clothes next to plain dark cotton clothing; long braids hanging down the Indians' backs and black bonnets on the Amish women. Perhaps they sat around this fire as night came on, with the smoke swirling upwards, the only light coming from the moon and stars, silence surrounding them. They became friends in the process, and Rhoda was always the first to get fresh juneberries.

These stories about how a Midwest pioneer befriended people from many different backgrounds and races with a generous, spunky and faith-filled spirit continue to influence my life. She modeled ways to persevere during the many seasons of my own life.

"You see, there are all those early memories; one cannot get another set..."

—Willa Cather

rhoda's roots

R hoda Ann was born to Isaac and Elizabeth Hostetler Kauffman in Reedsville, Pennsylvania, March 16, 1874, during a full moon. Her ancestry in the United States dated back to 1736, when Jacob Hochstetler and Anna Lorentz emigrated from Switzerland, sailing on the "Harle" from Rotterdam with Ralph Harle, shipmaster. It is interesting to note that the ship's record did not list the women or children, so Anna Lorentz was not listed, but her father, Johannis Laurentz, age 40, was.

Rhoda Yoder on her farm.

Jacob's last name was spelled three different ways: Hochstetler, Hostedler, Hofstedler. He was 32 years old when he came to America. He and the Lorentz family landed in Philadelphia Sept. 1, 1736. At that time, it took about six weeks to cross the Atlantic Ocean. Robert Louis Stevenson once described his experience upon landing in America:

> "There was a babel of bewildered men, women and children. They were crowded thick, heavy and rank with the atmosphere of damp clothes. There were hundreds of people and tons of luggage. It was a tight jam … mass of brute force and living obstruction. People pushed, elbowed and ran. Children fell, were picked up and rewarded with a blow. One child lost her parents, people rushed by as she screamed shrilly."

I wonder if Jacob and Anna found their first day in America likewise traumatic. This migration from Europe was one of the first wave of Amish immigrants to come to America. The Amish were a part of the Reformation in western Europe in the 15th century, when many questioned the connection between the Mother Church (Roman Catholic) and the state. Being a citizen automatically made one a Catholic. The Lutheran withdrawal was the largest split from the Catholic Church and the Amish the smallest and most conservative. Thousands of Anabaptists (most of them followers of Menno Simons, from whom "Mennonites" draw their name) died as martyrs rather than recant their beliefs. Others fled to America, as did Jacob and Anna Hochstetler.

beginnings...

Jacob and Anna were Rhoda's great-great-great-great-great-grandparents. The family stayed in Pennsylvania many years before Rhoda was born, March 16, 1874. She lived with her family in Reedsville, Pennsylvania, in the Big Valley, until she was 14 years old. The Big Valley is a beautiful valley about 30 miles long, nestled between two ridges, Stone Mountain to the west and Jack Mountain to the east, with Reedsville centrally located. Large trees filled the valley and covered the mountainsides. There was no shortage of wood for building or fuel.

Logging trails wound around the mountains.

Rhoda Yoder's birthplace, Reedsville, PA.

Pearl Street, Reedsville, Pa.

Seit 35 Jahren sind unsere Geschäfte mit gutem Erfolg gekrönt; dieses liefert den besten Beweis, daß unsere Ware von guter Qualität ist und wir ehrliche Geschäfte verrichten. Wir haben keine Agenten, sondern verkaufen direkt an Konsumenten; dadurch ersparen wir denselben den Profit der Agenten und Händler. Wir sind die größten Fuhrwerke- und Pferdegeschirr-Fabrikanten der Welt, die ausschließlich an Konsumenten verkaufen. Unsere Ware wird auf Probe versandt; sichere Ablieferung garantiert. Wir fabrizieren mehr als 200 Arten von Fuhrwerken und 65 verschiedene Sorten von Pferdegeschirren. Unser großer Katalog enthält eine vollständige Liste und wird auf Anfrage frei versandt.

ELKHART CARRIAGE & HARNESS MANUFACTURING CO., ELKHART, IND.

No. 654—TOP BUGGY WITH AUTOMOBILE SEAT, BIKE GEAR AND ⅞-INCH RUBBER TIRES

Preis.
{ Bar mit der Bestellung vollständig mit Deichsel und ⅞ Zoll garantierten Gummireifen......$71.00
{ C. O. D. vollständig mit Deichsel und ⅞ Zoll garantierten Gummireifen....................$73.00
Auf Wunsch liefern wir dasselbe mit regelmäßiger gear mit hohen Rädern anstatt bike gear.

No. 654 ist eines der besten, von uns hergestellten Stile bike gear top buggies. Es ist mit unserm neuesten Automobilsitz versehen, der geräumig und bequem ist. Wir wissen, daß dieses Buggy in seiner Konstruktion und Material durchweg so gut ist, als ähnliche, welche von andern für volle $25.00 mehr verkauft werden als von uns. Auf jeden Fall wäre es uns angenehm zur Prüfung und Bestätigung zu versenden. Sollte der Käufer nicht in jeder Hinsicht zufrieden sein, kann er dasselbe auf unsere Kosten zurücksenden.

BODY,— Derselbe ist durchweg vom besten Material und mit Automobilsitz versehen. Hat einen guten hohen Rücken und ist sehr bequem. Body ist 22 Zoll weit und 56 Zoll lang; aber wir liefern auch einen 24 Zoll Body, wenn ein solcher vorgezogen wird.

GEAR. — Römisches bike Muster mit staubfreiem Bell Kummet, long distance Achsen. Oel temperiert offene Hauptfedern; der Länge nach mit Eisen beschlagen, mit Bolze und Koppel gut befestigt; Bailley body loops clipped to springs; full circle rear king bolt fifth wheel; roller rub irons; Fernald rasch stellbarer Koppler. Schaft, regelmäßiges bike Muster, hergestellt aus bestem Wallnußholz; volle Glanzleder = Verzierung. Wir liefern Deichsel als Zugabe zu Schaft für $5.00 extra.

Räder. — ⅞ Zoll banded hub mit ⅞ Zoll garantierten Gummireifen. Schraube an jeder Speiche. Wenn gewünscht, liefern wir Sarven Patent Räder. Wenn anstatt ⅞ Gummiräder, 1½ Zoll Räder gewünscht werden, ist der Preis $5.00 höher.

Verzierung. — Dunkelgrünes Tuch für Sitz. Auf Wunsch liefern wir auch dunkelblaues Tuch oder Whipcord. Beide, Kissen und Lehne sind mit Federn ausstaffiert. Für $3.00 extra verzieren wir den Sitz mit Leder anstatt mit Tuch. Der Boden ist mit Brussels carpet belegt; auf Wunsch belegen wir denselben auch mit einer Gummi-Matte; Rubber boot, um den hinteren Teil des body zu decken. Sprißleder.

TOP. — Leather quarter, mit schweren Gummi Seitenvorhängen und Schußdecke. Wenn ein offener Treibwagen gewünscht wird, kann der top entfernt werden. Für $7.00 extra liefern wir full Leather top mit Leder bedeckten bows. Auf Verlangen liefern wir anstatt drei, vier bows.

Farbe. — Body, schön schwarz. Gear, New York rot, schön gestreift. Auf Wunsch liefern wir auch dunkelgrün oder treffen irgend eine Veränderung in der Farbe.

In Briefen nenne man diesen Kalender.

Black buggies moved west to Nebraska.

The Shawnee Indians would come down into the valley. They were friendly and enjoyed hunting and fishing with the white settlers.

In 1888, Rhoda traveled with her parents, Isaac and Elizabeth Hostetler Kauffman, and three younger brothers, Joe, John and Samuel, to Bertrand, Nebraska. One reason for moving was a church split over the color of the buggy they drove—the black buggies moved west and the white buggies stayed in Pennsylvania. Another reason may have been the lure of the West and almost free farms following passage of the Homestead Act in 1862.

Rhoda was 18 when she married John H. Yoder in 1892. They farmed successfully in Nebraska for several years with sufficient rainfall and good prices for their wheat. This area had wide-open prairies with few trees or rivers. Did Rhoda and John think of the beautiful mountains and plentiful wood back in Pennsylvania?

In Nebraska, sod houses showed creative use of materials available. Pioneers first plowed the sod with hand-held plows behind horses, about 2½ inches deep and 12 inches wide. Prairie sod was quite pliable. Next, they cut with a spade a piece twice the length of the width, or 24 inches. They laid it like brick, making a 24-inch wide wall. Sometimes they plastered the inside walls to make the house more comfortable. The men constructed the roofs in various ways, depending on available wood. They often laid sod to make grass roofs. Sod homes were wind-resistant and fireproof, though inhabitants occasionally saw snakes hanging from the ceiling.

From 1874-77, swarms of grasshoppers plagued farmers in Nebraska. They darkened the sky, even blocking the sun. The grasshoppers stripped the crops down to the bare stalks.

Years of very dry weather followed the grasshoppers, with little or no rain at spring planting time. To add to farmers' woes, prices went down. Corn that had sold for 27 cents per bushel in 1894 went down to nine cents per bushel in 1896.

The church had another split, adding another reason to move. This time the dispute was over whether men's shirts should be blue or white.

dakota bound

In the late 1800s, people in Nebraska started moving back to Pennsylvania, or to Kansas, Michigan or North Dakota. In 1904, the Yoders chose North Dakota. This was only 15 years after North Dakota gained statehood in 1889; before that, both North and South Dakota were Dakota Territory.

In 1904, Rhoda and John Yoder moved north with her parents, Elizabeth and Isaac Kauffman, in an immigrant rail car. John's brothers, Dave, Mike and Sammy, moved also. This rail car carried Rhoda and John's two children, 10-year old Edna Elizabeth and 8-year old Isaac Thomas, household furnishings, farm equipment and some cows, chickens, pigs, sheep and horses. Did hay and straw last for the journey? Did the cows ever get out to graze? Did the family sleep on their straw-tick mattresses? Did the swaying, creaking rail car and the noise of the steel track bother them? How often did the steam engine break the silence of the prairie with its whistle? Did the chickens wake them at dawn and the cows moo to be milked?

They rode as far as the rails went north, to Knox, North Dakota. Rhoda's parents settled there. John and Rhoda moved by horse and wagon 14 miles further, to Wolford, North Dakota, about 35 miles from Rugby, North Dakota, the geographical center of North America, where east meets west and north meets south.

The prairies of North Dakota were quite desolate, nothing but earth and sky. For miles, you could see the tall prairie grass blowing in the wind, like ocean waves. Emily Dickinson once described how "the wind rocked the grass." In some parts of the state with sufficient water, the grass grew as tall as the Indian ponies. There were very few trees and rivers though some water collected in sloughs in the low parts of the rolling hills. It took an adventurous spirit to move to North Dakota at the turn of the century. There was also beauty in the prairie, as this poet noted.

Sky-Mountain

Prairie land is golden,
Airy, wide.
The sky our only mountain,
We, inside.
Who would choose a small land
Where the hills,

Steadily asserting
Granite wills,
Narrow all horizons,
Stand apart?
Ah, my golden prairie,
In the sky-mountain's heart!

—May Williams Ward

One reason for moving there was the lure of homestead lands. The Homestead Act of 1862, signed by Abraham Lincoln, stated that any adult citizen or intended citizen who had never borne arms against the United States could apply for 160 acres of public surveyed land. If a person built some kind of structure on the land and lived in it at least two weeks each year for five consecutive years, the land was theirs. The filing fee was $18. The Homestead Act ended in 1934. A later law allowed owners to add to their land if they planted tree claims on a quarter.

Indians could not apply for homestead land. Was it because Indians were not considered "people" or had the Indians borne arms against the United States? Foreigners could apply if they were considering citizenship, but not the Native Americans already here. Nearby, cheap land was available. The sale of Indian land began in 1904.

Rhoda and John wanted a place of their own to raise their children. They homesteaded 160 acres, a quarter of land, on a farm one mile west of Wolford on the top of a rise, or rolling hill. They could see for miles around. To the east was lake bottom land known as Grass Lake that had been a dry lake for many years, though later there were wet years when it could not be used for farming. The family's first shelter was a one-room house, about 15 by 15 square feet, made of sawn wood.

It was not easy settling in, getting shelter for their animals and food for the winter. One of the first things they had to do was drill a well.

I remember Grandma Rhoda talking about "witching for water." A person would find a Y-shaped branch and then walk over an area while holding the branch. It would make a sharp turn down over water, sometimes with such force that one could not keep it from turning. We called this voodoo, or The Force, or a "gift" that a certain person had, though now there is a scientific explanation for it. After finding a water source, settlers used windmills or hand pumps to bring the water to the surface.

John and Rhoda worked hard to set up their homestead. They were determined and independent pioneers. The first year, John worked for another farmer. He had a bed in the granary at the farm. In 1906, another baby, Aaron, was born, adding one more person to the 15-by-15-foot cabin.

John H. Yoder and Rhoda Yoder's 15 x 15 foot homestead house, 1904.

tragedy strikes

In 1907, only three years after moving to North Dakota, at the end of harvest in September, John cut his leg with a blow from an ax while chopping wood. The leg became infected. John did not go to a doctor right away, and by the time he did, he had what they called blood poisoning. The doctor in Rugby recommended amputation but John did not want that.

After struggling painfully for three months, John died of blood poisoning Dec. 21, 1907. He and Rhoda had been married only 14 years. She was left alone with three children: Edna Elizabeth, age 14, Isaac Thomas (Tom), age 12, and Aaron Kauffman, age two, in the cold North Dakota winter. In addition, Rhoda was pregnant with their fourth child. Five months later, on May 8, 1908, Fanny Mae was born. She had black hair and a rather dark complexion.

At the time, women hid their pregnancies well. They had never heard of maternity clothes, but just made their loose dresses a little bigger and put on a large dark apron. They often stayed home, isolated, for months before the baby was born. Years later, Fanny Mae would write in her journal:

> "My thoughts go back to Christmas past, to my very own mother Rhoda. The Christmas before I came into this world was probably my mother's very worst Christmas. Four days before the holiday my father, John Yoder, died. My mother was all alone on the desolate prairie with three children, Edna, Tom, and little two-year-old Aaron. And me, in her belly, just in the middle of formation. Five months later on May 8, 1908, I came into this world, never to know my father."

Hand drawn family portrait: Rhoda's parents, Elizabeth and Isaac Kauffman, Rhoda (with baby Fanny in the womb), and son Aaron.

How does a 33-year-old pregnant widow get through the long winter months after her husband has died? How could she not worry about the little new life within her? It was hard enough for a family living on the prairie, with a man as the head of the household, to make a living and have enough to eat and a place to live. The Yoders were outgrowing their little wooden shelter. Even with an addition built on, it was too small.

Before John died, however, they had made the plans and collected material provisions to build a larger house, two stories with bedrooms upstairs. The house was built in 1908 but there is no record of how. The Amish do "barn raisings" so easily so perhaps the community built this house in a similar fashion.

After John's death, Rhoda's parents, Isaac and Elizabeth Kauffman, came to live with her for a while. Their German names were Grosmutter and Grosdade.

The new baby (De Bup) did not nurse well. Maybe her mother was working too hard—milking those cows and moving into a new house while trying to nurse a baby had to be daunting. Grosmutter would crush crackers into a bowl and add warm coffee and milk to feed the baby. Maybe that is why my mother, Fanny Mae, liked coffee so well. (In later years, Rhoda would leave the coffee she made in the morning on the back of the old black kitchen stove and Aaron and Fanny would

Rhoda's second house, built in 1908.

finish it when they got up.) Grosmutter would also feed the baby "bry," a thin cooked pudding with a little brown sugar sprinkled on top. Is it any wonder the baby no longer craved her mother's milk?

Fanny Mae remembers that her Grosdade was always protective of her. Sadly, four years later, he too died.

Fanny's older sister, Edna, got married at 18 to Eli G. Hochstetler. Soon her brother Tom married Emma Witmer. Now Rhoda lived alone with her mother and the two younger children, Aaron and Fanny Mae.

an independent woman

Rhoda—or as many fondly called her, Rodie H—was an independent and resourceful woman. (The "H" was *not* Rhoda's middle initial, but rather her *husband's* middle initial. This was to differentiate between several John Yoders in the community. Consequently, "Rodie H" was John H. Yoder's wife.) As a young widow with two little children, Rhoda managed the homestead farm.

When she opened the barn door, each cow went to her station in the barn. Rhoda milked the cows by hand, wearing long skirts and balancing on a one-legged wooden stool. Holding the milk bucket between her knees and pushing her head into the cow's flank, she squeezed with both hands and "stripped" each teat into the metal bucket. The milk stream pinged into the foamy milk.

Rhoda knew her Guernsey cows. She named each one and talked to them. One she called Bessie. Rhoda was gentle with her cows and did not excite them with loud noises.

After milking, Rhoda strained the milk through

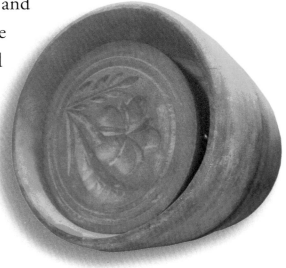

Butter press.

a clean cloth and let it cool as the rich cream rose to the top. She skimmed off the cream to make into butter and the young calves lapped up the leftover skim milk.

A wooden churn made the butter. Aaron and Fanny would trade off turning the churn, counting the rounds, until the cream separated from the buttermilk to make the butter. Rhoda used buttermilk in cooking and as a drink. On top of each round of butter, about a pound each, she made a small design with a wooden press and then put the butter in a fancy, round, cut-glass covered dish.

Once a week, Rhoda took the extra cream, eggs and butter to Wolford. She had what she called her cream route. She would drive around Wolford in the buggy and at each house on the route, Aaron and Fanny Mae took the sparkly glass jars full of rich cream, sealed with a little round paper top, up to the door and brought back last week's empty jars with change for payment inside them. They were delighted when part of the change was pennies because Rhoda allowed them to keep the pennies. She took the extra cream to Clark Hill's grocery store and exchanged it for the few groceries she needed.

The grocery store had large barrels of flour, sugar and salt. In the fall when the wheat check came in, Rhoda would buy 200 pounds of flour, 100 pounds of sugar and 10 pounds of coffee beans to prepare for a long, cold winter. She also bought seasonings and tobacco. (Rhoda and her mother smoked corncob pipes. Later Rhoda learned of the dangers of smoking and made a pact with her son Tom to quit if he did.) She also bought five cents worth of pink peppermints and at Christmas time hard ribbon candy. If any money remained, she bought raisins, prunes and dried apples.

Rhoda never charged at the grocery store though she did at Jimmie Gardner's drugstore, the blacksmith shop and the hardware store. Every fall when she sold her wheat crop, she went around and paid off debts.

Each spring, Rhoda ordered 100 fluffy yellow chicks from a catalog. When the chickens were big enough to eat, she taught Fanny Mae how to butcher them. A large stump outside was the execution spot. With one foot, Rhoda pinned the legs of the squawking chicken to the stump. She held the head with one hand and used the other to cut the neck with a sharp knife. The beheaded chicken flopped around on the grass. After it stopped moving, Rhoda dunked the whole chicken in a bucket of boiling water, which made the feathers easier to pull off. If she kept the chicken in the hot water too long, the skin tore off, too. (Why are chickens with no feathers called

C. E. HILL

WOLFORD, NORTH DAKOTA

Penick Syrup

Clark Hill's Grocery Store, Wolford, ND.

"dressed" chickens?) After she removed the feathers, Rhoda pulled out and discarded the insides of the chicken, except for the heart, liver and gizzard. She pulled the skin from the gizzard without disturbing its smelly insides. Finally, she thoroughly washed the chickens and they were ready to cook or sell. Each week, Rhoda prepared five or six chickens for her regular costumers. They sold for 75 cents or a dollar each. She was an expert at searing the freshly cut-up chickens and finishing them in the oven. There is a skill to cutting up a whole chicken correctly, too.

Rhoda never had indoor plumbing but instead a small two-hole outhouse. The Sears catalog supplied the paper (the black-and-white pages were softer than the colored ones). The seats were especially cold in the winter when the snow drifted in. No one lingered in the privy. The odor was not good.

The old black kitchen stove had a reservoir on one side that supplied hot water. The children carried in water after pumping it from the well, and carried out the slop pail when it got full. Everyone took a bath on Saturday night in a round galvanized tub in front of the stove. Fortunate were the ones who bathed first and got the clean water.

Rhoda had a rigid washboard to wash clothes. She boiled white clothes to keep them white and she hung the clothes outside to dry, even during winter, when the clothes would freeze stiff. This made it easier for them to finish drying indoors. They smelled wonderfully fresh.

The kitchen stove served other purposes, too. Rhoda wrapped heated bricks in towels to warm beds or buggies. Children dressed in the morning in front of the stove when the bedrooms were freezing cold. Occasionally, Rhoda carried in tiny blue premature piglets to set beside the stove, warming them up to squalling pink.

Mattresses were made of straw ticks or feather ticks, with down feathers used for pillows. Rhoda was usually ready for bed by the time the chickens went to sleep. Fanny Mae always slept with her mother while Aaron slept in a small bed in Rhoda's room.

Rhoda used kerosene lamps sparingly. The glass chimneys would get black soot on them and Rhoda washed them in soapy water every Saturday. The wicks had to be trimmed. Gas lamps made brighter light and she hung them above the table. She pumped air into them to make a broader bright light. Children never lit gas lamps, as they could be dangerous.

The farm supplied most of the family's needs. Rhoda had a garden west of the house where she grew potatoes, corn, peas, beans, cucumbers, red beets, onions, lettuce, carrots, squash and melons. Some vegetables, like tomatoes and cabbage, she started in the house to set out later. She also had patches of asparagus, rhubarb, strawberries, gooseberries and flowers. I remember especially cosmos and zinnias.

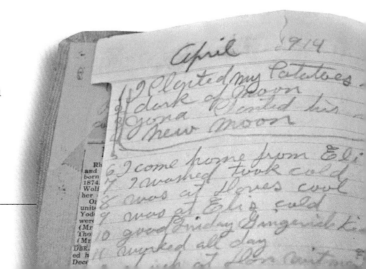

1908 Almanac, the year Fanny was born. Rhoda planted her garden by the phases of the moon, according to the almanac.

The growing season is short that far north. Summer days are long, lasting from 4 a.m. to 10 p.m., and usually sunny. Gardens grow fast. Rodie H. always had food to share.

She planted her garden by the phases of the moon, probably checking the "Farmer's Almanac" for this information. That which grew above the ground—like beans, lettuce, cucumbers and corn—she planted between the new moon and the full moon, the first and second quarters of the moon. That which grew underground — like potatoes, beets, carrots and turnips—she planted in the third and fourth quarters when the moon is waning. I remember her hoeing dirt up around each corn plant to conserve water. Rhoda had a scarecrow in her garden near the corn and pumpkins to discourage birds from eating her harvest.

She used manure from her horses and cattle as fertilizer and practiced good farming methods like crop rotation. An old newspaper described plowing with horses. Twenty miles a day is a full day's work. A field on a quarter section could be a half-mile long. A complete round with a plow would total one mile. The horses needed rest after a round. It was hard work.

Rhoda saved seeds from the best plants for the next season. She stored root vegetables in a dirt cellar. Later, she canned dozens of quarts of fruits and vegetables and put up a lot of jam. In the winter, the family cut large chunks of ice from the sloughs and stored them in straw underground. These ice blocks would last well into the summer, when they could make homemade ice cream.

food preparation on the prairie

Rhoda made "schmierkase," or cottage cheese. She let milk sit until it clotted in a warm place on the back of the old black cookstove. Then she drained the clotted milk through a clean cloth, rinsed it and added salt and a little sweet cream. She ate schmierkase on freshly baked homemade bread with chokecherry jelly. Great-Auntie Maud and Tom's wife Emma made large rounds of orange cheese, similar to cheddar. That was a real treat.

Rhoda made waffles in a waffle iron on the cookstove. You had to turn the iron to bake both sides of the waffles. She filled the squares on the waffles with sweet cream butter and brown sugar. It was delicious.

Cornmeal mush could make a complete meal. Rhoda cooked cornmeal slowly for hours in a black kettle over low heat. The family ate the mush in bowls with milk and a little pat of butter melting in the middle, then poured and molded what remained into bread pans. In the morning, it was sliced, fried slowly and eaten with syrup for breakfast. (Now we call this "polenta".)

When the weather turned cold, families got together for butchering. They used nearly all parts of the animal (as someone said, "with the exception of the squeal!"). They made liverwurst, a good breakfast meat to be eaten with pancakes and syrup. They made sausages by thoroughly scrubbing and cleaning the intestines, inside and out, until they were thin and white, and filling the casings with ground seasoned meat. Some parts, like ham and bacon, were smoked in a smokehouse. They rendered the fat

Rhoda's recipe for white bread.

Gram.

To Betz —

White Bread
2 cups hot milk
¼ " sugar
¼ " shortening
2 tbls. salt

"2 cups warm water
2 yeast cakes
about 10 or 12 cups flour.

heat milk, add shortening & sugar & salt, add yeast to warm water, let rise & when milk is only warm add to yeast, mix with 4 cups flour & beat hard, let rest 10 min. and work in flour until (over)

stiff, grease dish, and let stand in sunshine or warm place 1 hr, then knea' again, & let raise again 1 hr. form in 3 or 4 loaves & let set 10 min, then put in greased Pans & bake 45 - 55 min. good good — Don't forget to make fried bread for dinner !

oven temp 350°

and made it into lard. The men butchered beef for steaks, roasts and hamburger. The women used the bones to cook up hearty soups and the mincemeat to bake into pies. On butchering day, everyone stayed around afterwards for a big supper.

In the winter, they made snow ice cream, gathering fresh white snow in a bowl and adding thick sweet cream and sugar. You had to eat it fast before the snow melted.

Mothers baked bread several times a week, as they did not have plastic bags or freezers to keep it fresh. Children often came home from school to the smell of freshly baked bread. They ate thickly sliced bread with butter and jelly or syrup or apple butter.

Rhoda looked forward to dandelion salad in the spring. She gathered the greens before the dandelions bloomed. Dandelion salad is similar to spinach salad, served with a warm tangy dressing and garnished with sliced hard-boiled eggs and crumbled bacon.

rhoda and the chippewa indians

There was not much fresh fruit in North Dakota but some berries, like chokecherries and wild plums, grew wild. The Chippewa Indians, from the Turtle Mountains 30 miles north on the border between United States and Canada, came down on horses to sell firewood and also brought buckets of juneberries.

At first, when she was alone, Rhoda was afraid of the Indians. She may have heard of the Sioux uprisings in Minnesota around that time. However, she probably also remembered the friendly Shoshone Indians who came down from the mountains in Pennsylvania to fish and hunt with the settlers. I wonder how aware the Chippewas were of the sale of Indian land that started in 1904.

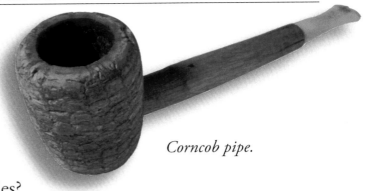

Corncob pipe.

Despite her fears, Rhoda, with her mother, would sit around the fire at night with Chippewas, both parties smoking and gesturing to make a deal. Would it be fresh bread or ham or chicken or even garden produce to trade for fresh juneberries? I wonder, as the smoke curled upwards, if they ever saw the northern lights (the aurora borealis, a spectacular show of red, green, white and purple lights, moving in waves up and down, that can be seen best in North Dakota, Alaska and Michigan).

After a smoke, the Indians and Rhoda must have felt good, because they became very close friends. Rhoda got the first ripe juneberries each year.

One year, the Indians brought a cornhusk doll for little Fanny Mae. "One time," Fanny Mae wrote in her journal, "they came on my birthday, May 8, and gave me a nice beaded horseshoe with the year 1908 beaded on it." Once Rhoda traded a whole ham for 20 gallons of juneberries. Juneberries (saskatoons, the Canadians call them) grow wild and are similar to blueberries.

One year when the Indians came down, a woman with a new baby came along. That night it began to snow and blow. Rhoda felt sorry for the young mother and her tiny baby and let them sleep in the upstairs bedroom. The next day, however, Rhoda was dismayed to find fleas upstairs. She had to get rid of the fleas in the straw mattress, which in those days meant she probably had to burn the mattress. Fanny wrote in her journal: "[The fleas] were all over. We had to carry buckets of water to throw around and kill them!" In the morning, the young Indian woman took food for the journey.

A favorite meal that used fresh juneberries we called "bruckles." Rhoda would break day-old bread into a large bowl, pour on sweetened milk and top it with juneberries. To this day, our family enjoys this cold summer soup with other fruits, as well.

rhoda provides for others

During hard times on the prairie, large families with ragged children, some even with men at the head of the household, stopped by unexpectedly. Rhoda knew they were hungry and soon prepared a large meal with smoked ham or home-canned beef and a wide choice of vegetables from the cellar. They probably finished with raisin cream pie or sauce. (Did you ever taste plum sauce or homemade butterscotch pudding topped with real whipped cream?) No one left hungry. Rhoda had food for everyone, and never accepted government aid, even though she qualified with her low income.

Rhoda knew and befriended people of other races. A black man named Henry Rhodes traveled north after the Civil War and sometimes lived with them. He worked occasionally as a barber in Wolford. He usually brought oranges when he came out from town, which was a real treat.

Rhoda's recipe for raisin cream pie.

The children called him "Uncle Hemmy." He would entertain them and one of the children even picked up his Southern drawl. He attended church with them and may have been the first black man baptized in the Dakotas.

Besides Indians coming to visit, gypsies traveled in covered wagons across the country. They would set up camp a half-mile from the Yoders' place for a few days and would come over to see Rhoda. She was a little apprehensive about them because gypsies sometimes stole things and she was afraid they would steal her children. However, Fanny said, "They have enough children of their own!"

Rhoda made the children stay in the house with the screen door locked when she dealt with the gypsies. They tried to find out where she kept her money by offering her trinkets or beads and saying, "We give, now you give." She gave them food rather than lead them to where she stored her money. She offered live chickens, smoked meat, eggs and bread. In a few days, they would move on.

a homestead neighbor from chicago

A wealthy Chicago man, Carl B. Bernsten, a Norwegian, had homestead land across from the Yoder place. He came out each summer to live in his claim shack the required two weeks for homestead land. Each summer, "Uncle Carl" would bring Fanny Mae a doll with real hair and sleeping eyes. Until then, she had only rag dolls and the cornhusk doll from the Indians.

Old china doll.

Mr. Bernsten with Twila and Iva Stoll.

When Fanny was 14, Rhoda suggested to Mr. Bernsten that maybe Fanny Mae was too old for dolls. So he gave her a light brown registered Jersey calf. They named her Flora Dora. (Who thought of that name?) When this calf became a cow, Rhoda would let Fanny keep every other calf, and Rhoda took every other calf in return for providing food and shelter for them. By the time Fanny Mae got married, she had four Jersey cows from this first calf.

Mr. Bernsten also sent large wooden boxes of used clothes to Rhoda. I remember an adult's winter coat with a real fur collar made into a child's coat. We still have a large wooden box with my father's name engraved on it that had contained the used clothes from Mr. Bernsten.

The claim shack could not have been very comfortable for Mr. Bernsten, a hefty executive who wore three-piece suits with starched white shirts and ties. Sometimes during these summers, he came to live with Rhoda's family in the big house across the road.

Fanny Mae remembers how Mr. Bernsten loved the big vegetable garden. In the morning, when he got up, he would empty his white chamber pot, and then

Fur trimmed coat from Mr. Bernsten's box.

wash it out in the stock tank where the cows drank. He would then proceed to the garden and fill the pot with fresh vegetables for the day.

This did not please the woman of the house. When he was not around, she would discard the vegetables and then gather more in her clean garden bucket. Fanny wrote: "I was always glad to see him come and mom was glad to see him go!"

amish artistry

Rhoda did not make the colorful, beautifully pieced and finely stitched quilts that some Amish women did. She did not have time for that. However, she sewed all the family's clothes, even for the men and boys.

Rhoda sewed for other people as well, especially men's coats and suits. Fanny remembered Rhoda staying up late with the kerosene light, sewing those clothes for others. She also made heavy bed comforters. Rhoda had a treadle sewing machine that she pedaled with her feet. Her thimble had an open top.

Amish houses were stark and simple—no curtains, no pictures on the walls, no photographs and no art, except their beautiful quilts and dishes.

Above: Rhoda's open-ended thimble.
Amish quilt design.

Many Amish quilt designs were outstanding. Women made quilts with scraps left from their dresses. Since the Amish never allowed plaids, stripes or prints of any kind for their clothes, no quilts were made of printed material. Every quilt had some black in it, since much Amish clothing was black. Other colors used were dark red, bright blue, deep greens and shades of purple. Patterns were usually simple shapes cut out of cardboard and handed down to the next generation. The three oldest patterns the Amish used were: Sunshine and Shadow, an arrangement of small squares in light and dark colors; Diamond in a Square, made of large pieces with intricate patterns quilted on them; and Bars, long bars in solid colors with borders and designs quilted on them.

Why do many Amish have these splashes of beauty and color in an otherwise plain, dark environment? Some among them had artistic talent they could not express because of strict religious rules. However, a quilt was not merely artistic, but functional as well, and their religion allowed this. Girls were encouraged to have several quilts made before they got married. Quilts were a necessity for keeping warm, and as a bonus were a spot of beauty in a world of hard, repetitious work. Most of a woman's labor did not last. Food was eaten, clothes got dirty, and floors had to be swept again. However, quilts became a thing of lasting beauty, a creative accomplishment adding color to a gray world. Quilts became their works of art.

Many Amish immigrants brought their dishes along when they crossed the ocean. Rhoda had a beautiful set of English bone china. The pattern is Adams Rose, hand-painted in bright colors. The last time I checked, the plates were worth $130 apiece and a cup and saucer $75. Family members still have pieces of this china. The bold colors must have stood out amidst the otherwise somber, dark colors in Rhoda's home.

Another source of color and design was the very fine cross-stitching on the pillowcases. The women sewed this stitching across one thread at a time. One of Rhoda's pillowcases has pink cross-stitch showing three small pots of flowers, her initials and "1894."

Rhoda's dishes, Adams Rose china from England.

rhoda as midwife

Rhoda was also a midwife and medicine woman. Fanny remembered Rhoda chanting over home brews made from the roots of wild plants she had dug up, but she could not recall the words Rhoda used. Some of Rhoda's remedies were simple, like a piece of fat tied over a cut to draw out infection or a sliver. She warmed cooking oil and dribbled it into an ear for earaches, while toothaches got peppermint oil. Warm salt water was gargled for sore throats. Rhoda made a bitter tea called boneset and everyone got a dose of castor oil in the spring. She got some medicines from traveling salesmen who would trade for food and shelter. One of these was a dry-goods peddler, Mr. Blocher. He was an honest man, a member of the Dunkard Brethren people. He peddled dry goods and sewing supplies and was sure to make his rounds before winter set in.

Rhoda delivered many babies at home. The only preparation for this was boiling water and clean towels. Folks had large families and often, even at night, a buggy would drive into Rhoda's yard and she would go to help with a birthing, coming home the next day. Even though she delivered many babies, or maybe because of potential risks she knew about, she insisted her daughters go to Rugby to a hospital for their deliveries. Another midwife, Mary Baker, lived in Wolford. Rhoda delivered the Amish babies and Mary delivered many of the non-Amish. I wonder if she delivered Rhoda's children, Aaron and Fanny.

Rhoda never talked to Fanny about where babies come from. Fanny was puzzled about where her mother got the babies she brought to other families. Fanny remembered: "One day when Rhoda came home from a delivery, she said she had brought a baby to their house. I could never understand where she got the baby and why she did not leave one at our house. When my brother Tom and Emma had a new baby boy, I was very surprised, and this time they had to go to a doctor. That was a puzzle to me, too. What did the doctor do and why could Mom not bring us a baby, too? I was so ignorant! Why didn't someone tell me?"

"One time mom went to deliver a baby to a family that had one every year. When she came home, she brought their year-old baby home for a week. Sadly, we could not keep this cute little guy with the red curls."

Another time when Rhoda delivered a baby, she needed to stay overnight. She had to sleep in the couples' bed with them, the mother sleeping in the middle! This family had a baby every year. Children were a gift from God.

transportation

A horse and buggy worked well in the summer. Some buggies even had heavy cloth tops that could be lowered for a cooler ride in the warm months. (However, you could get a bit dirty after a rain on dirt roads since the wheels spattered mud on you.) When the weather got a little frosty, the buggy tops went back up. In North Dakota, winter temperatures could drop to minus 30 degrees or even 40 degrees below zero. Snow could begin as early as October and did not melt until late spring. Snow would drift high, even over the fences, blocking the roads for weeks. No trains or mail came in.

Another winter conveyance was the cutter, a small covered sleigh—really a wooden box fastened to runners, with benches inside for seating—pulled by two horses. A small, round, pipe-like stove provided cozy warmth. It was exhilarating to glide on top of waves of snow, right over the fences. However, if soft snow pockets caused the horses to go down, the cutter would tip and then the driver would have to shovel the cutter out. The children inside were afraid of the burning ashes from the little stove.

food for the soul...and body

Rhoda always got to church on time. At an Amish worship service, there were two sermons, preached in High German, though at home the Amish spoke mostly Pennsylvania Dutch, a German dialect. Prayers were silent. Church met every two weeks, alternating among members' homes. Many homes had a wall that would swing up and hook at the ceiling to make a larger room for church. The

German Hymn book.

men hauled benches from home to home in wagons. In the summer, they often met in a haymow—the new-mown hay must have smelled wonderful.

The sermons lasted for more than two hours. Children often got tired sitting on the backless benches, listening to sermons in a language they did not understand. About midway through the preaching, the women would serve large, soft sugar cookies to the children.

After church, everyone stayed for a meal, which always included home-baked

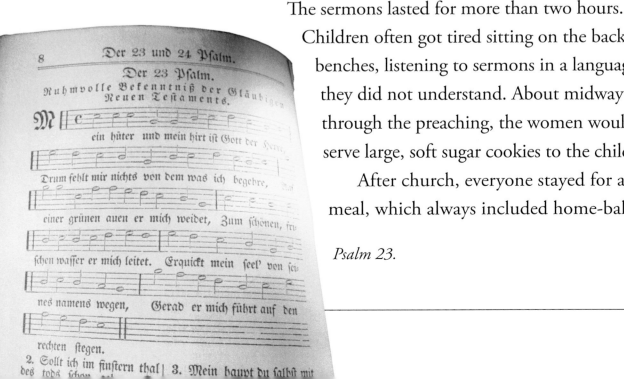

Psalm 23.

bread with apple butter or jam, red beet pickles and other kinds of pickles, and sometimes white bean soup or homemade noodles to fill them up. There were half-moon pies made with dried apples. The women served the men first, then the young folks and children, and themselves last.

As a girl, Fanny said, "I always enjoyed going to church (not that I understood the preaching) but afterwards we could cuddle the babies and play church. After my nephew Melvin was born, I had my very own baby to care for after church."

From her grandmother Ann Hostetler, Rhoda received a wonderful leather- bound hymnbook, written in German, with two clasps to keep it closed. Inscribed inside is: "I present to Miss. Rhoda. Ann. Kauffman. From. Mrs. Ann. Hostetler. Received the 3 of March in the year 1888." (The publication date is 1871, in Philadelphia.)

In this hymnbook, the Psalms come first and included beside each Psalm a simple melodic line for singing. The staff has no clef signs, only a "C" symbol, meaning 4/4 or "common time." The Amish do not sing in harmony as Mennonites do. The last part of the hymnbook has no musical lines at all, just lines of words to sing. You need to refer to the front to find the tune for each song.

Since the Amish church met every two weeks, Rhoda began letting Fanny and Aaron attend the Mennonite church and Sunday school (which was in English) on the other weeks. Eventually, she allowed them to go every Sunday and several years later, she transferred her membership there also.

Years later, I remember sitting with Grandma Rhoda in a simple, white clapboard Mennonite church. The men sat on one side and women on the other. The children usually sat with the women. Parents maintained strict discipline. They took noisy children out and spanked them.

My Grandma Rhoda was rather short, with soft, saggy skin. She was plump, with a soft, cushiony feel. I enjoyed leaning against her. Rhoda also kept pink peppermint candies in her pocket for us. Mom usually tied a penny in the corner of a cloth hankie for me to take for the Sunday school offering. My first teacher was my Aunt Edna, up in the front coatroom, where we sat under the hanging coats. Every Sunday, she would give us a colored 2X4-inch picture of the Bible story. These were greatly treasured. She was a wonderful aunt, married to the minister, Eli G. Hochstetler.

At a children's meeting at church, Fanny first realized that there was something more important than just this life to live for. In a granary about a mile from their home, revival meetings took place. Fanny remembered: "We walked to hear this great preacher. That night he preached 'hell fire.' I was afraid. My mom consoled me. She said I was too young to understand. If I was a good little girl, God would take care of me."

Fanny wrote, "One night we came home from church after dark. We were afraid to go in. Rhoda lit the kerosene lamp and went all over the house and looked under the beds and all, and found everything OK." What would she have done if someone had been there? She had no telephone, no police and no nearby neighbors.

romantic postcards

Rhoda was a young widow of 33 when John died. Various men pursued her, but she seemed satisfied with her single life. Rhoda did not need a man to tell her what to do.

I traced the trail of one man who courted Rhoda, from some one-cent picture postcards she kept. Banks McDonald from Alexander, North Dakota, sent many to her. He sent a card to her on Dec. 14, 1910, that read: "Tell me do you still love me in the same old way I do you and a little better" (no punctuation marks). This would have been three years after she became a widow.

One card had a bird's-eye view of Alexander, North Dakota, which is no longer on the map. He sent a brief message, which said, "from your Irish lovey dove."

Romantic postcards sent to Rhoda from Banks McDonald.

Above and facing page: Romantic postcards sent to Rhoda from Banks McDonald.

(How did they meet? He was not German—he was Irish.) One card simply said, "Write me a letter." Several had the message written on a mirror backwards so she had to look in a mirror to read them. These are beautifully illustrated, colored cards.

Another card sent from a man in Oregon read, "I have worked for two months for $25." That would be less than 50 cents a day.

Rhoda had only about three years of formal education. Her friends probably had similar schooling, according to the way they spelled words on these cards: "Youens" for you; "Fryday" for Friday; "fue" for few; "bee" for be; "beried" for buried; and often "Roda" for Rhoda.

Although Rhoda had very little formal education, she owned books, received magazines, almanacs and catalogs, and wanted her family to have more education. She kept a precise record of her farm income, the weather, the price of food and everyday happenings in one journal. Rhoda read to Fanny and Aaron every night before they went to bed. She read in English, not in German. Rhoda gave Fanny a Bible with both English and German. Sometimes Rhoda would read a verse in German and Fanny would read it in English.

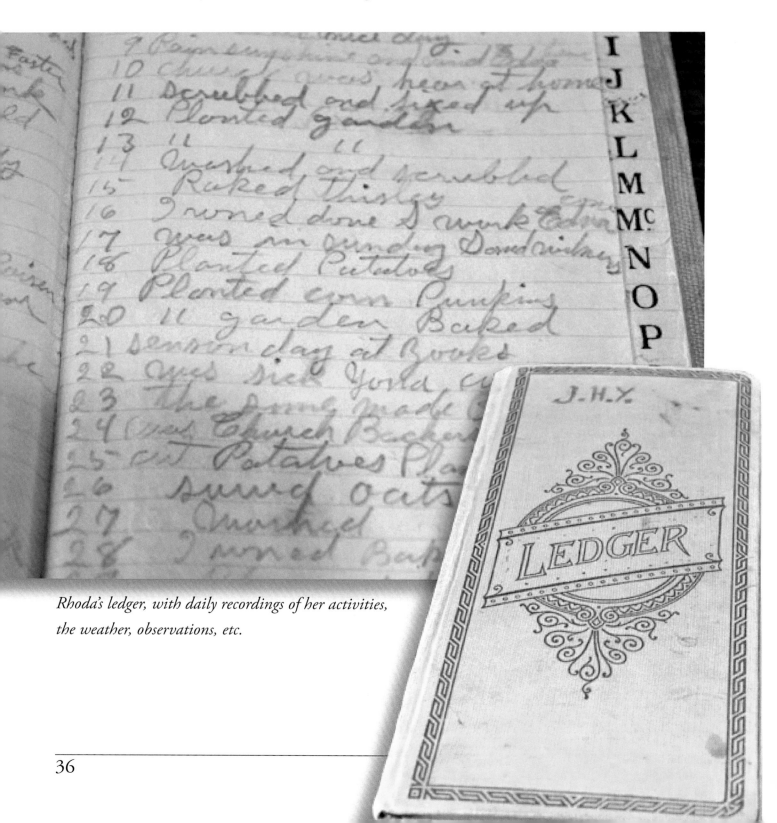

Rhoda's ledger, with daily recordings of her activities, the weather, observations, etc.

19 ...... head ? in field
20 Edna head in field
21 awful sundy in field
22 rained after noon
23 raind again
24 is foggy lvls like my
25 ? was at Reeses all night
26 Edna was her
27 ? drilled 15 acres of oa
28 ? Plowed was cold
29 ? Plowed was nice w
30 ? washed and made g

school days

T he children had chores every day. They washed and dried the dishes and got up early to feed the calves and slop the pigs before they went to school. Later, each of them had their own two cows to milk. Rhoda always went with them carrying the kerosene lamp, as it was still dark. They enjoyed a good breakfast of fried mush and liverwurst, and packed their dinner pails with homemade bread and syrup, but hardly any fruit. (That is why they needed a dose of castor oil.)

Aaron and Fanny Mae walked the mile and a half to Wolford for school. Fanny wrote, "I remember my first Christmas program, held in the Lutheran church.

Fanny's first and second grade school in Wolford, 1915-1916.

Surprisingly, my mother let me be in it. I was supposed to be an angel. My long braids were unbraided and my hair was in waves with a shiny halo over my head. I was about the happiest kid there! I can still see the large Christmas tree with real wax candles, and popcorn and cranberry strings."

Fanny and Aaron were the only Amish children in the school. Fanny was ashamed of the black bonnet her mother made her wear to school. Children teased her about it. When she arrived at the corner fence post near the school, Fanny would tie the bonnet to the post and pick it up after school. This worked quite well, as Aaron kept the secret.

Fanny wrote in her journal, "One day it rained and rained most of the day. My older brother Tom came to pick us up after school. I had to tell him about my bonnet still hanging on the post, soaking wet! He laughed. After my punishment (whatever that was), I was allowed to go without the bonnet. I could wear a men's red scarf or go bareheaded. I was happy!"

"A school friend, Alpha Dunham, lived south of town. We walked the first half mile together after school. One night she asked me to stay overnight. I had never been to an 'English' home, the beauty of big mirrors, nice pictures, pillows all around and curtains thrilled me. They must be very rich. When it came time to go to bed, I wanted to go home. I had never been away from home at night, and always slept with my mom. I cried and cried. Mrs. Dunham would have taken me home but her driving horse was out in the pasture. About midnight, I finally went to sleep and was fine the next morning. The next week Alpha went home with me. I suppose she was impressed with our plain home. We had a good evening playing and went to bed upstairs in our spare room. Again, I could not go to sleep, creeping quietly downstairs, my mom tucked me in with her. When my mom got up the next morning, I crept upstairs and crawled in bed with my company. She never knew I left."

"One summer my cousin from Wisconsin came to visit. We were threshing oats and we wanted to play in the oats bin. Mom said No, but when she went to town, we went in the oats bin. That evening when we undressed there was oats in our shoes. 'Did you go in the oats bin?' 'No, No' we said. We had gone in and she knew! She spanked us both, not so much for disobeying her, but for lying to her. I cannot remember any other spankings we got."

"My grandmother knit wool stockings for us and we wore long underwear and heavy clothing in the winter to school. We carefully folded the long underwear at the ankle and pulled brown stockings over them hoping classmates would not see that we had long underwear on. We always had modest dresses with long sleeves. We nearly roasted at school and got sleepy."

Fanny remembers: "We memorized long poems in school. One was The Village Blacksmith, by Henry Wadsworth Longfellow. I could stand up in front and recite the entire poem."

The Village Blacksmith
Henry Wadsworth Longfellow. 1807-1882

UNDER a spreading chestnut tree
The village smithy stands;
The smith, a mighty man is he,
With large and sinewy hands;
And the muscles of his brawny arms   *5*
Are strong as iron bands.

His hair is crisp, and black, and long,
His face is like the tan;
His brow is wet with honest sweat,
He earns whate'er he can,   *10*
And looks the whole world in the face,
For he owes not any man.

Week in, week out, from morn till night,
You can hear his bellows blow;
You can hear him swing his heavy sledge   *15*
With measured beat and slow,
Like a sexton ringing the village bell,
When the evening sun is low.

And children coming home from school
Look in at the open door;   *20*
They love to see the flaming forge,
And hear the bellows roar,
And watch the burning sparks that fly
Like chaff from a threshing-floor.

He goes on Sunday to the church,   *25*
And sits among his boys;
He hears the parson pray and preach,
He hears his daughter's voice,
Singing in the village choir,
And it makes his heart rejoice.   *30*

It sounds to him like her mother's voice,
Singing in Paradise!
He needs must think of her once more,
How in the grave she lies;
And with his hard, rough hand he wipes   *35*
A tear out of his eyes.

continued

Toiling,—rejoicing,—sorrowing,

Onward through life he goes;

Each morning sees some task begin

Each evening sees it close;   *40*

Something attempted, something done,

Has earned a night's repose.

Thanks, thanks to thee, my worthy friend,

For the lesson thou hast taught!

Thus at the flaming forge of life   *45*

Our fortunes must be wrought;

Thus on its sounding anvil shaped

Each burning deed and thought!

Fanny listed the 22 business places in Wolford in 1915. The blacksmith shop was the first business when you turned off the road into Wolford. I well remember looking into the door (as Longfellow had), fascinated with the pounding on red hot metal.

As I read the words to this poem these many years later, I am amazed at the parallels to Rhoda's life.

Fanny wrote, "My brother Tom helped me with math. I hated the subject. He would help me with a problem, explain it to me and then tear up the paper. I was very disappointed, as I still could not work them. However, my brother Aaron could! He let me copy his! This did not help me. In spelling, I nearly always got 100, and Aaron could hardly spell at all. [In typical Fanny humor, she would say, 'But words are more important than numbers!'] He could write his spelling words at home but in school, he could not hear the teacher. My brother, Aaron, was hard of hearing, not a very healthy child and missed a lot of school. I caught up to him and we were in the same grade. He was sick a lot and never did finish common school. I graduated from eighth grade school when I was fourteen, the first one to graduate from my family. For graduation, my sister made me my first white dress with a collar and big sash tied in the back!"

In her journal, Fanny remembers the losses in her life. "I used to feel sorry for my brother Aaron. We were very close to each other. I do not remember that we ever fought, always shared half an apple or an orange, even half a stick of gum." Aaron died when he was only 23, of pneumonia and brain fever.

fanny's childhood memories

Fanny does not remember a lot of playing she did as a child. Fanny and Aaron played quietly because their grandmother, Elizabeth Kauffman, was sick and did not like noise.

Fanny Mae's Uncle Joe gave her a baby lamb to feed on the bottle. All summer, the children petted the lamb, played with her and fed her. The lamb was Fanny's pride and joy and followed her everywhere. She finally had a pet of her own. One morning in late fall, while Aaron and Fanny were having their breakfast of coffee soup, her big brother Tom and Uncle Joe carried something through the kitchen and down into the cool cellar. "It was my pet lamb, all butchered and ready to eat." Fanny said, "I never ever once took a bite of it."

Fanny had a cousin, Lena Yoder, who was the same age. Her family used to come to spend the day and visit. Fanny remembered: "One time when it was time for them to go home, Lena and I decided to hide so she did not have to go home. We crossed the road and hid in the Bernsten shack. We heard them call and call, but we did not answer. Finally, they decided to go home without her.

Aaron (Rhoda's son), Rhoda Yoder, Elizabeth Kauffman (Rhoda's mother), Tom (Rhoda's son), Fanny (Rhoda's daughter), Emma (Tom's wife), Glen (Tom and Emma's baby).

Were we happy! We planned to sleep together and have lots of fun. Coming out of hiding too soon, they turned around and saw us. We both got our paddling, not for hiding, but for lying and saying, we did not hear them. Lena had to go home. When Lena was 8 years old, they went to Michigan to visit and Lena got the measles. She got a 'back set' and died within a week. So there went my best playmate too."

Fanny's older brother Tom and his wife Emma lived across the road with three babies, Glenn, Mable and Violet Joy, who were very special to Fanny Mae. Tom gave Fanny a little rocker with carved spindles to rock "her babies." Perhaps all

those dolls from Mr. Carl B. Bernsten encouraged Fanny's love of babies.

Fanny Mae loved to take care of her sister Edna's children, Melvin, Rhoda, Perry and Emery. Melvin was only six years younger than Fanny Mae, but he was "her baby." Fanny wrote, "When he was born, I asked, 'Could I hold him?' 'Yes, if he cries at night,' they answered. They brought him to me when he

Left: Rhoda's daughter Edna, with husband Eli Hochstetler. Below: Hochstetler car and barn

fussed. I fed him a raw apple! I never knew when they put us both to bed." Edna lived eight miles away but came home with horse and buggy once a week and stayed all day.

When Melvin was six years old, Rhoda gave him their horse, Bingo. He was gentle to ride and drive. Fanny remembered: "That was tough for Aaron and me. We had another horse but never another Bingo." By that time, Melvin had three siblings and all three or four kids could ride on Bingo's back at the same time.

In 1918, Edna was involved in an accident in a new Model T Ford when it overturned on a poor road. At the time, she was pregnant with her fourth child. Her doctor confined her to bed because of concern for the unborn baby, then three or four months along. Like Zechariah in the Bible, Edna was unable to speak for the duration of the pregnancy. She needed help with the housework and care of the other children, ages one to four. Edna and Eli lived on a farm and had a hired man who also needed meals. Fanny had just turned 10 and had little experience in housekeeping but she liked children very much. When Eli asked if she would like to come and stay with the family, she said, "I jumped at the chance!" She thought being away from home would be an adventure.

Every morning, she would check in with Edna in bed. She would ask directions with a slate in hand for Edna to write on. Fanny had little experience in cooking, but proceeded to follow directions. "I did the best I could. I fried eggs for breakfast and fried potatoes for supper!"

Once after Fanny had asked about putting salt on several foods, Edna finally wrote, "You should put a little bit of salt on every food you cook." Fanny later discovered salt did not work well in coffee or on rhubarb.

On Friday, a hired girl came and washed clothes, baked bread and cleaned the house. Fanny said, "The days she came, I only played with the children all day long!"

Months later, after the birth of Edna's baby Emery, Edna's speech, like Zechariah's, miraculously returned.

the twice paid farm

Rhoda lived through the extremities of the prairie weather: rain, hail, drought, blizzards and dust storms. Having met the requirements for owning the homestead quarter, Rhoda decided to mortgage the home quarter to buy the quarter across the road. She had written a check for two thousand dollars to the banker. The honest banker had promised he would take care of it all for her.

One fall, after Rhoda had the wheat crop harvested, she hitched her horse to the buggy and took Aaron and Fanny Mae with her over the dusty road to Wolford. They went to the elevator first to get the wheat check and after that to the blacksmith shop, Mr. Anderson's hardware store and the drugstore, to "settle up" their accounts. At the drugstore, Jimmy Gardner always gave them a gift. Once it was a lovely china dish and once it was a set of six silver spoons.

Rhoda must have felt light and happy. Now she finally had enough money to make the last payment on the quarter she bought. It was a good feeling to know she had enough to pay it all.

To her dismay, Dick Sugdon, the banker, left town taking the money that many pioneers had paid for their land. In her words: "He pocketed it all and skipped the country." No one ever heard from him again.

Rhoda had to start all over and pay for her land for the rest of her life. It was the "twice paid" farm. How many chickens, eggs, cream and bushels of wheat did it take to pay for it again?

Eventually, the farm was paid for a second time. Rhoda even bought a car, a dark green coupe with thin tires. Rhoda had to crank it in the front to start it. The car had a stick shift. The grandchildren rode on a shelf in the back.

Rhoda was accustomed to horses that responded to her voice. The first time she drove the car up to her shed, she evidently could not remember how to stop it. In vain, she yelled, "Whoa! Whoa!" The car did not stop, of course, and she went right through the wall.

fanny mae and abie j.

When Fanny was 14, she became aware of boys. The children often played "Hide and Go Seek", hiding all over the farm, when the families got together for dinner. Soon one of the Stoll boys, Abe, started hiding with that pretty Fanny Yoder. I wonder how many others knew about this handy arrangement to become acquainted.

Abe Stoll grew up in a large family. His ancestors came from Indiana. His father was a farmer, skilled carpenter, bricklayer and horse trainer. When the family home became too small for all the children, he decided to build a new one. Their little old red house had leaking walls. In the small upstairs room, two of the small boys would crawl into a low bed with a straw mattress and feather tick cover and the older boys would shove them under their bed. A stovepipe ran up through their room to help

14-year-old Fanny with friend Sadie Yoder.

keep it warm. In the morning, their dad would rap on the pipe to get them up. One morning, the stairwell was full of snow. Before the boys could come down for breakfast, their dad had to shovel the snow out.

After the new house was built, one of Abe's first memories was when he needed to find a hammer. His father had locked the large chest where he kept his tools, so Abe decided to pray for a hammer. When he opened his eyes, he saw a beautiful butterfly and he chased it around the new house. In the soft dirt of the yard, he saw a stick poking through. Thinking he could

Abe Stoll at age 16.

reach the butterfly with the stick, he pulled it up. It was a hammer. This was an answer to prayer.

Abe started school when he was five, anxious to learn to read. His first trips to school were in a billy goat cart that his brothers had made. Later they drove to school in a buggy pulled by a horse, old Cougar. Abe recalled that on one trip to school in the winter when he was older and driving a load of younger siblings to school, the horses took off with the sleigh, out of control. Concerned for the safety of the little children, Abe started tossing kids out on the snow banks. When he looked back, there were kids lining the road for half a mile. No one was hurt.

Blizzards can come up swiftly on the prairies. Abe wrote: "My brother and I were digging tunnels in a huge snow bank some distance from the house. Suddenly we could not see the house or any building. Fortunately, my brother Joe had seen us playing in the snow-bank earlier. He came out and rescued us. That storm was a three-day blizzard. Three days later, we found our horses and got them to the barn. We worked with a currycomb and a stick to get the snow out of their thick hair."

Abe and Fanny Mae.

When Abe was in the sixth grade, he bought a suckling black Percheron colt for three dollars at a neighbor's sale. Abe's father also bought, trained, and sold registered black Percherons, sometimes as many as 50 at a time. He gave Abe another colt. Now Abe had a team of black Percherons. He trained them well and by the time he was in eighth grade, Abe could drive his younger siblings to school with his team.

On the hillside in the pasture, Abe and his brother saw a badger. That evening, his brothers decided to drown the badger out of its hole. They hauled a barrel of water out to the pasture on a sled but

were unable to drown the badger, so they decided to dig him out. Although they dug as fast as they could, the badger dug even faster. Suddenly they came upon two tiny baby badgers. They were so small they could fit on a page of the Sears Roebuck catalog. Abe fed the badgers with a spoon until they could drink from a pan. They grew to be very

Top: Abe's first car.
Right: Abe at age 19.

large badgers. Abe would walk on the prairie with his pet badger, which loved to dig for gophers.

At 14, Fanny started working in a cook shack, a traveling kitchen that followed the threshing rigs. These rigs moved from farm to farm, harvesting grain from the grain shocks (the bundles that haulers brought in from the fields).

Early in the morning, you could hear the threshing rigs' steam engines whistle, signaling the beginning of a day's work. On a clear day, the steam from four or five threshing rigs rose above the prairie. Operators vied to see who could be first to get their steam up and blow their whistle.

Hired cooks served breakfast first, before the crew of men began threshing. Daylight comes early in North Dakota, about 3 a.m. The cooks had stacks of pancakes piled high for the men and, later, stacks of plates as well. When Fanny Mae started helping her mother in the cook shack, she could sleep in until the men came for breakfast. Her bed was a shelf-like place above the table area. After the men ate their fill of pancakes, Fanny would get up to wash the high stack of dirty dishes.

Abe remembered hauling water out to the men working in the field. When he was older, he hauled the grain in a farm wagon to the grain elevator in town. His team knew the way without him steering them. Many days, he would walk beside the wagon to keep warm. He wore a sheepskin coat, but seldom wore shoes.

Fanny Mae also worked for a while for one of Abe's older brothers. One Sunday, he told Abe he could bring Fanny home from church. Abe cleaned his buggy and curried his registered black Percheron team, and went to church that evening. Fanny was happy to ride with him. They had a good time.

When Rhoda heard about it, she said, "Fanny, you are too young. You are only 14." Several years later, Rhoda came to Abe and said, "If you can get your horse and buggy ready for Sunday evening, I will let you bring Fanny Mae home." This was the first of many trips to the hill west of Wolford. Soon Abe's horses knew the way to Rhoda's house without him directing them.

Abe had plenty of competition, however. One night after service, Abe pulled his team up to the church door, ready for Fanny to come out. He waited and waited. Finally, he left the team standing and went in to find Fanny. There she was talking to another boy. Meanwhile, someone outside whistled at his horses and his beautiful black Percheron team took off across the prairie, into the night, without Abe.

Abe recalled in one of his journals that a skunk got into the church one night and sprayed the floorboards. No matter what they used, they could not get rid of the odor. They finally had to remove the boards and put new ones down.

We used to tease our parents, calling them Abie J. and Fanny Mae. Abe sent Fanny beads and a few trinkets but Rhoda would not let her keep them. Rhoda did not allow Fanny to keep gifts from boys, so Fanny hid them. Later in life, Abe always signed his name "A.J. Stoll."

When Abe was still a teen, he told a friend he wanted to be a medical missionary, but he never had the opportunity to go to school. He had to work on the farm during those years.

marriage and family

Fanny recalled: "Abe asked me to marry him, so I thought, fine, that's all I had in my head those days anyway, get married and have lots of babies which I loved."

"I was in church and Abe stood up and asked the church if he could marry me!" They got married October 30, 1927, when Fanny was 19 and Abe was 23. They had a big turkey dinner for all the guests. Taking two best friends with them, they went on a three-month honeymoon, first to Niagara Falls and then to the beautiful valley in Pennsylvania where Rhoda was born.

Abe and Fanny eventually bought the farm across the road from Rhoda. Mr. Bernsten had moved an old section house out to the farm. Abe added a barn and other necessary buildings. Abe and Fanny's first two children, Iva Belle and Twila Mae, enjoyed life on the farm, their first home.

316¾—(Rev. Code 1943—Sec. 14-0320).   KNIGHT PRINTING CO., FARGO, N. D.

Marriage License

STATE OF NORTH DAKOTA,

County of __Pierce__ } ss.

To any person authorized by law to perform the marriage ceremony, greeting:

You are hereby authorized to join in marriage __Abraham J. Stoll__ ,
of __Wolford, North Dakota__ , aged __22 years__ ~~who has~~ ~~been~~
~~divorced~~, and __Fanny May Yoder__
of __Wolford, North Dakota__ , aged __19 years__ ha~~s~~xxx ~~been divorced~~;
~~the Application for the within license was accompanied by the physician's certificate and the laboratory state-~~
~~ments as required by sections 14-0312 and 14-0314, Revised Code of 1943~~; and of this License and your Certificate
you will make due return to my office within ~~five days~~ __thirty__ ~~after the date of solemnization of the Marriage. No Marri-~~
~~age may be solemnized under this license unless so solemnized within 60 days of the date hereof.~~

Dated at __Rugby, N. Dak__ this __24th__ day of __October__ , 19__27__.

(SEAL)

__J. T. Berdahl__
County Judge.

Certificate of Marriage

I hereby certify that the persons named in the foregoing license were by me joined in marriage at
__Lake View Minnonite Church__ , County of __Rolette__ ,
State of North Dakota, on the __30__ day of __Oct__ , 19__27__.

In presence of

__Aaron Yoder__

__Edna Stoll__

Witnesses.

__Eli T. Hochstetler__

__Bishop in Minnonite Church__
Official Title—Ecclesiastical Body

Address

Abe Stoll and Fanny Yoder's marriage license.

When I was born in Rugby, North Dakota, Dr. M.C. Caul was my attending physician. At that time, they kept new mothers and their babies in the hospital for a week or 10 days. That seemed a long time to my sister, two-year old Iva. When we finally came home, Iva said, "She's not very purdy." My mother described me as "being all big eyes and big mouth and a pug nose on a round face. We loved her anyway."

Stoll—Y d .—Ab 1 Stoll and Fanny May Yode were married at the Lake View Mennonite Church near Wolford, N. Dak., on the evening of Oct. 30th in the presence of a well sized audience. E. G. Hochstetler offici-ating. May the Lord keep them safely throughout their entire life's journey.

Honeymoon trip to Niagara Falls. Abe and Fanny on the right, with friends "Coon" Yoder and "Toot" Beyler on the left.

Abe and Fanny's farm (the old Bernsten place) with vintage autos.

My parents were struggling to establish their home on the prairie and did not have cash immediately on hand to pay Dr. Caul's bill. He received the balance of his payment in the form of dressed chickens. Every time we went to Rugby, some freshly butchered chickens went along. I think he was sorry when the bill was paid! I was old enough to remember that I was "not paid for"—my parents teased me, saying they would give me back to Dr. M. C. Caul because they had not paid for me yet.

I attended school in Wolford in the two-story brick building with two classes to a room. My first grade teacher was Mrs. Platz. I remember the smell of the

Fanny with baby Twila.

oiled hardwood floors. We had signals for going to the bathroom, Number 1 and Number 2. I will not forget when I put up one finger for Number 1 and Mrs. Platz shook her head no. She probably remembers also, as there was soon a flood under my desk.

My third grade teacher was Miss Magdeline. Memorable that year was my first and, as far as I can remember, my last attempt at cheating. The seat beside me was empty, so I carefully wrote my spelling words on a small piece of paper and laid them on the seat. When my dear teacher called out each word, I double-checked to see if I had spelled it correctly. It might have worked except an eagle-eyed country boy with manure on his shoes saw it. He must have blabbed to Miss Magdeline. The next week, she walked around while calling out the words. (Did I not have an ancestor who had trouble spelling?)

Twila's school.

We had inkwells on each desk, small glass containers of ink to dip our pens into. It was too much temptation for the boy sitting behind me. He saw my long braids and dipped them in the inkwell. I think it was permanent ink.

8 years

Top: School picture
of Twila, age 8.
Right: Iva, Twila,
Joyce, and Ardys Stoll,
enjoying the snow.

I remember having a lot of fun in my childhood. Some favorite games were "Anti I Over," "Pump, Pump, Pull Away" and softball. In the winter, we played "Goosy, Goosy, Gander" and "King of the Hill" and made many snow forts for snowball fights. When we moved to town, we were free to play all over town. No one was worried about strangers.

One spring when the lilacs were very fragrant, I walked by a house that had huge lilac bushes all around the perimeter of the lawn. There were thousands of blooms. Knowing my mom loved flowers, I picked a large bouquet—no one would miss those few blossoms. When I reached home, I rushed in to give my bouquet to her but Fanny's first reaction was, "Where did you get those flowers?" After I told her, we walked silently back to the yard and I apologized for picking the flowers. Another lesson learned.

In the summer, we played paper dolls on the dirt floor of the garage. We put a large old blanket on the floor. We built many houses for the paper dolls, which we

"Lilac lesson."

cut all from the Sears Roebuck catalog. We dreamed of large houses, fancy clothes and beautiful people.

One Christmas, I wanted ice skates. I dreamed of a pair of girls' white figure skates. When I opened my package Christmas Eve, there was a pair of boys' secondhand black hockey skates. I was not too surprised because I had nosily burrowed through a closet and found my gift several days before. The skates worked very well on the frozen sloughs.

Another Christmas, I fared better when I got a child-size set of lovely Blue Willow china dishes. We spent hours having tea with them, evidenced by a few broken pieces and a cracked meat platter.

When we still lived on the farm, the haymow was a favorite place to play. We climbed a high ladder to a small shelf at the top of the haymow, which was filled with fragrant clover hay. We used to swing way out on a long rope, probably a pulley rope, and jump into a large pile of freshly mown hay. That was a thrilling ride!

Child-size set of Blue Willow dishes.

Iva and Twila on the farm.

My sister Iva really wanted to try the swing ride. She finally carefully climbed the long ladder but when she got to the top, she was afraid to jump. After several days of this, I got tired of seeing her never have the nerve to jump, so I finally pushed her. She narrowly hit the pile.

Top: Twila, age 1, and Iva, age 3. Above: John and Terrence, ages 1 and 3. Left: Joyce, age 3, and Ardys, age 1.

Another haymow memory is climbing as high as my cousin and I could, and sitting on a windowsill chewing wheat grain. If you chew wheat long enough, it becomes like gum. Years later, we found a baking powder can of wheat we had left there.

Iva described an old horse, Coon, we had when we were quite young: "We rode old Coon, a pokey old bunch of skin and bones who patiently allowed our childhood antics and went no faster than a half hearted amble regardless of all the 'Gitty-ups' and rib kicks."

Another source of joy was my first horse, Snickers. Iva had a horse named Tootsie. Her horse had been ridden before but Snickers was not trained to ride. My dad took me out to a plowed field so if I fell off it would be a softer landing. I fairly flew across the field, riding bareback and hanging on to the bridle, my bare feet digging into Snicker's belly. Later on, I remember the sound of her hooves pounding as we rode on the packed dirt trails around our farm, and her whinnying just for me.

One sad memory from childhood was when our dog, Jack, died. He was the dog who could go and fetch the cows for milking from the pasture by himself. My dad and I were swathing grain for harvesting. Dad sat on the swather while I pulled it with the John Deere tractor. Jack wandered in front of the swather and it cut off two of his legs.

Looking back, I was such a tomboy. I enjoyed working outside better than the chores inside the house. I helped Dad with the evening chores when I was about eight. After he milked the cows, he took the milk to the house and told me to finish feeding the cows their ground oats and then come for supper. After he left, I put my hand in the grain bin for another pail of oats. A rat trap was set in the grain bin and it snapped on my arm. I could not open the trap and I could not get loose because the trap was nailed to the wall so a rat would not haul it off. Finally, someone from the house stepped out, called "Supper!" and went back inside. Sometime later, they came out and called again and this time heard my cries for help. Those were long minutes.

When the cattle ate the pasture grass down, I herded cattle in the ditches around the farm. It must have been a boring job, but I do not remember being bored. I enjoyed sitting in the sun.

I remember walking the same road to school that my mother had walked. One fall, it was colder than we thought it was, and my nose and fingers got white from frost. My mother knew (probably from her mother) that you do not apply heat to frozen skin—instead apply something cold, even snow, to the area. Too much heat causes further injury.

Church was not only religion; it was our social life as well. We loved summer Bible school when we saw our friends every day. We memorized long Bible passages from the old King James Version that we would remember all our lives. During recess, we played softball as well as

Grandma Yoder with baby Joyce, both born on March 16.

other games. We sang our hearts out. At the end of Bible school, we had a program to show our parents what we had learned.

My father Abe attended Bible school one year at Hesston College in Kansas when we children were young. His small daughter wondered if he was going to be gone "a thousand years." That was the winter I remember tipping in the cutter.

Several years later, Joyce Eileen joined the family, born on Grandma Yoder's birthday, March 16. My dad wanted a son at each birth of his daughters. When the fourth daughter came, she went without a name for a whole month. Finally, they called her Ardys Joanne Stoll, so she had his initials, A. J. Stoll. I think they had given up on having a son. Fanny wrote, "We loved this little dark one anyway."

church call to casselton

In 1943, the Stoll family moved to Casselton, North Dakota, so Abe could serve the church there as a minister. During that time, they finally added two sons to the family, Terrence Abraham and John Mark. Although Abe never quite attained his boyhood dream of being a medical missionary, the eldest son, Terry, became a radiologist. When the youngest son, John, was born, I remember my father saying in a senatorial voice, "His name is John." I think he remembered Zechariah settling an argument by writing in his scroll, "His name is John" (Luke 1:63). John now teaches school in Montana, with a Native American population.

Abe and Fanny's eldest daughter, Iva, became a secretary and worked with the migrant population. She inherited Fanny's ability to piece and stitch beautiful quilts. The second daughter, Twila, became a teacher and librarian. The "purdy" third daughter, Joyce, works as a bookkeeper for her veterinarian husband and is also a cook extraordinaire. The fourth daughter, Ardys, a teacher, worked among the Métis people in Canada and inherited her mother's wonderful sense of humor as well as being a quilt-maker.

Fanny's door in Casselton opened even wider on Saturdays when she made her famous raised doughnuts. We seemed to gravitate to the aroma that floated out the door. She also made them for Mennonite Central Committee Relief Sales, the profits from which benefited Third World countries. One year, the last doughnut sold for $30. The next year, it came back to the auction, varnished and framed, and brought $50 more.

Fanny made quilts for each of her grandchildren and for the wedding of each child. Since she was born May 8, 1908, that made her 80 in 1988. On her 80th birthday, we hung her quilts around City Hall in Casselton and served a lunch with food similar to that eaten in 1908.

Fanny's hobby was

Grandma Fanny's raised doughnut recipe.

Raised doughnuts   Grams
dissolve 2 cakes yeast in 1 cup warm
water, set aside. 1 pt milk scalded, add
½ cup shortening ½ cup sugar, ½ teas nutmeg,
1 scant Tble salt, 3 beaten eggs, 2 cups flour,
when cool add yeast mixture and mix 4½
cups flour (more or less), knead to soft dough,
put in greased bowl + cover with towel. let
rise + punch down, let rise again + roll
¼ to ½ in thick, cut with doughnut cutter, let
rise, then fry in hot lard, turn once (over)

drain on paper towel, while still hot
Glaze with this.
1 lb. P. sugar
2 Tbls corn starch
½ cup water (more or less
vanilla.
dip doughnuts while still warm + drain
on pan, use glaze over until gone.
should make 3 doz doughnuts or more.

making quilt pieces, but she was also a peacemaker. The patterns of the quilts tell a story of the lives of pioneers. Fanny's quilts portray characteristics she had, like frugality. She always made do with what she had, using every scrap of material. Grandma Yoder said, "Waste not, want not."

The older quilts were like a family album. The quilt she made for me was the Flower Garden pattern. I can point to the pieces made from scraps of two dresses I got for my fifth birthday. The designs for quilts came from everyday objects the pioneers worked with. Some of the pattern names were Log Cabin, Grandmother's Flower Garden, Crazy Patch, Dresden Plate, Grandmother's Fan, Basket, Lone Star, Churn Dash, Tumbling Block, Friendship Quilt and Double Wedding Ring.

Here are few examples of Fanny's quilt patterns that do indeed make a statement about Fanny.

The Flower Garden pattern is reminiscent of the farm, where the road went around her garden of petunias, zinnias, marigolds and cosmos. She shared both

Grandma Fanny's quilt for Twila.

Top: Double wedding ring pattern. Above: Crazy quilt!

flowers and seeds with others. I never knew her garden used only by her family, which illustrates Fanny's hospitality.

The Dresden Plate pattern reminds me that dishes were also a spot of beauty in Fanny's life. She handed down the bright hand-painted English bone china dishes from her grandmother. The Dresden Plate design is fashioned after a popular china plate made in Germany in the 1700s and the pattern is also reminiscent of the design of a buggy wheel on Fanny's first courting vehicle.

Churn Dash or Monkey Wrench: As a handyman, Abe used many wrenches. He made the frames that held the quilt for stitching. In later years, he would figure the border patterns of the design so they came out square at the corners. He also helped mark the quilts for quilting. Churn Dash is another name for this pattern. Fanny made butter in a glass churn with the golden cream swirling around.

Double Wedding Ring: This beautiful design speaks of 58 years of married life for Abe and Fanny, and the six children who followed. Fanny used this design, which has 1,584 pieces, to make a quilt for a granddaughter.

Crazy Patch: This is probably one of the oldest quilt patterns. Frugality is noticeable here. Every snippet of material is used, even leftover embroidery thread, which makes the decorative stitches around each crazy piece. These stitches even had crazy names, such as turkey tracks. Crazy quilts got their name because there is no set pattern. I wonder if they also helped those pioneer women from going stir crazy in winter when a blizzard kept them home for two weeks. This was a good prescription for cabin fever.

These are illustrations of frugality, care of family, hospitality, friendship, love of nature, beauty, and sociability in all of Fanny's quilting.

Fanny and Abe served the church in Casselton, North Dakota, for 35 years. When a beautiful 1886 stone Episcopal Church in Casselton sold, Abe was instrumental in buying it for the Mennonite congregation. The men of the church decided to put a basement under the church for classrooms and fellowship hall. It had to be dug mainly by hand because of the thick stone walls. When they got to

Above: Casselton Mennonite Church, watercolor by Ladd Bjorneby. Left: Church bell. Right and following page: Stained glass windows in the Casselton church.

the middle of the room, they encountered a huge rock, with no way to remove it. After a few consultations and a few prayers, they decided to dig a hole, large enough in which to roll the rock. They were successful. Someone downtown, two blocks away, said people felt a tremor.

Abe gave several sermons linking the symbolic beauty of the stained glass windows to the life of the church. The beautiful rose window at the front has the Greek letters IHS in the center, meaning Christ. Many years ago, most people could not read or write. Christian symbols can be found in the catacombs in Rome. Later, church windows with symbols and pictures would tell the Bible stories. For example, the beautiful sheaves of grain reminded viewers of the story of Ruth. Abe's favorite window was the pelican feeding her young by plucking the feathers from her neck until it bled, a nurturing symbol. The cluster of grapes tells the story of

the young men entering the Promised Land or the communion wine. The dove tells the story of the Holy Spirit descending on Jesus at His baptism.

The church building is now on the National Register of Historic Places and serves as the Casselton Heritage Center, functioning as a museum and a venue for events and programs, including a Smithsonian exhibit in 2009.

Abe and Fanny spent their retirement years doing volunteer work in many places in the United States. During this time, they went to Europe, where they participated in communion in a cave where Menno Simons had been. They spanned the years of horse drawn buggies on the plains to planes flying across the ocean.

Sanford Eash wrote a series of four articles about Abe and Fanny in *Purpose* magazine in February 1979. In summation, he wrote:

"Abe and Fanny never seemed concerned with impressing themselves, or anyone else for that matter, with their own importance. But the longer we knew them, the more we realized these delightful people possessed a deep inner strength and beauty. … Abe and Fanny came from homes, which valued a simple faith and hard work."

Shortly before she died, Fanny said, "The fall weather looks old and brown, just like me, old and brown." The day she died, she said to her nurse, "I'll see you in heaven."

rhoda's legacy

Generations later, we remember Grandma Rhoda and the twice-paid farm. Rhoda was among the pioneers who succeeded in establishing a home on the prairie. People moving West had skipped over the treeless plains and settled the West Coast, believing this was not a profitable area to locate. There were no trees for building homes or providing fuel. They believed nothing would grow here except grass. Perhaps Rhoda persevered because she was of the prairie: the winds, the dust, the grass, the snow, the sun, the windmills, the 15 x 15-foot house with three children, the broad sweep of the beautiful prairie under the blue sky.

Rhoda lived as some people strive to live now. It was a simple life, a life lived off the land. She was a hard worker. She disciplined her children. She was stubborn yet pliable, willing to try new technology. She told her daughter Fanny, "Most important to me is that my children keep the faith." Rhoda was a well-known figure in the community. She was a philanthropist, although she would not have known the term. She had real, undeniable courage to live on the bleak farm alone, raising a family and paying for the farm twice.

Rhoda passed on concise moral maxims to us. "A stitch in time saves nine." "All that you do, do with your might; things done by half are never done right." "Don't count your chickens before they're hatched." It is remarkable how those pop up in your mind for the rest of your life. These were formative in our character development.

Rhoda moved back into the original 15 x 15 foot homestead house..

Did Rhoda ever ponder the verse, "Go ye into all the world and preach the gospel to every creature?" (Mark 16:15) The world came to Rhoda's door. She fed the hungry, healed the sick, cared for the needy, taught her children, loved and provided for her family, shared what she had, loved her neighbors, and identified with minority groups.

Rhoda's son Tom moved the little pioneer house to Wolford and added a small lean-to addition for a kitchen and bedroom. Rhoda planted flowers and vegetables around the house. She walked across the block to get water at a pump. Evidently, people still sought Rhoda for healing in 1944 for she wrote in a letter to Fanny, dated Sept. 17, 1944: "Wednesday Simon came for me that Joe Graber had ivie poisoning and got something else with it. Anyway, I helped him, the next day he was better."

In her last letter to Fanny, Rhoda wrote, "I did not know I had dropsy. My heart is a little flutry this evening. I carried a five-pound bag of sugar from the grocery store. Seems I cannot do anything anymore, made me a bunch of high pillows. Tom brought me some water. I do not need much as I have rainwater." Fanny came from Casselton to help care for her mother.

Rhoda died at age 71 in the little 15 x 15-foot house she and John built as pioneers in 1904. Many people remember the plucky pioneer widow who always had food and a welcome for all. Her family remembers the "twice-paid farm" and "her children rise up and call her blessed" (Proverbs 31:28).

Yoder.—Rhoda Elizabeth Kauffman, ...ughter of Isaac and Pa., March 16, 1874; was born at Reedsville, ford, N. Dak., July 7, 1945, died at her home in Wolford, N. Dak., July 7, 1945, of coronary heart disease; aged 71 y. 3 m. 21 d. On Jan. 19, 1893, she was married to John H. Yoder, who preceded her in death Dec 21, 1907. To this union four children were born: Edna L.—Mrs. Eli G. Hochstetler, Mylo, N. Dak.; Thomas I., of Wolford; Fanny Mae—Mrs. Abe J. Stoll, Casselton, N. Dak.; and Aaron K., who preceded her in death June 1, 1928. In youth she accepted Christ as her Saviour and united with the Old Order Amish Mennonite Church. In 1924 she transferred her membership to the Mennonite Church and remained a faithful member. She always attended church and Sunday school when health and circumstances permitted. In her teen age she moved with her parents to Bertrand, Nebr., where she lived until 1904, when she with her family moved to Wolford, in which community she lived the remainder of her life. Besides her three children, she leaves to mourn her departure, 3 brothers (Joe, Lebanon, Oreg.; John, Oroville, Calif.; and Samuel, of Lebanon), 13 grandchildren, 8 great-grandchildren, and many other relatives and friends. Funeral services were conducted July 10, at the home of Thomas Yoder and at the Lakeview Church by John Stoll and Edward Hershberger. Text, Rev. 14:13.

Dellis, age 2.

epilogue

I married Dellis Schrock of Iowa City, Iowa. We met at college as editors of the yearbook. After two years, I taught school and Del finished college at Goshen, Indiana. We got married on August 23, 1953, and Michael, our son, arrived nine months and two days later, an important detail in 1954.

I have never met a harder worker than Del. He thrived on doing two jobs at the same time. Once I pointed out that he held five chair positions simultaneously: mayor of Casselton, church council chair, head of the English department at South High, president of the North Dakota Council of Teachers of English and president of Phi Delta Kappa. And how can I forget… head of the Schrock household, too. Del taught English and creative writing in Fargo, North Dakota, for 40 years. He always said he wanted to be able to work as long as he lived, and die with his boots on.

Dellis and Twila, 1952.

Dellis and Twila Schrock family, 1965.

We enjoyed a family of four children, Michael Lewis, Deirdre Ann, Joan Marie and Elizabeth Jean. They married Erin Geiser, Tomas Albrecht, Don Woodward and Marvin Slabaugh, respectively.

Del and I lived a happy, rewarding life with our family for 54 years. Tragedies mark all our lives. For me, sadly, Dellis died while working on a house damaged by Hurricane Katrina in Louisiana (with his boots on!). Two days later, a truck struck and killed our son Michael while he was in Fargo helping with preparations for his dad's funeral.

"What matters most is how you walk through the fire," Garrison Keillor once said.

Michael, an architect, designed the first LEED school in Minnesota, at Twin

Lakes in Elk River. He had recently become principle and co-owner of the firm LSA Designs. He enjoyed his new office on the 18th floor, overlooking the river in downtown Minneapolis. Mike was a compassionate man and many valued his friendship. Relationships he formed in high school, college and church, in the neighborhood and at work, continued throughout his lifetime.

A friend from Goshen wrote a eulogy to Mike: "If anyone was blessed with a

Michael, Deirdre, Elizabeth, Dellis, Twila, Joan, at Long Lake in MN, 1972.

combination of personal intelligence, charisma, humor, motivation, determination and good looks, it was Mike. He had every reason to have a big ego with his successes in life, but instead he genuinely cared about other people. This made him a much classier guy in every sense of the word. As old memories of Mike, without warning or cause, appear to me, one thing is certain… He will be truly missed."

My life is filled with blessings as well.   Our grandchildren are Zachery Tomas Albrecht, Atlee Abraham Geiser Schrock, Brittany Rose Albrecht, Haven Avery Geiser Schrock, Laurel Mae Schrock Woodward, Linnea Schrock Slabaugh, Twila Mae Albrecht, Landon Lewis Slabaugh, Ardys Ann Schrock Woodward, Anya Elizabeth Slabaugh and Chloe Juana Schrock Woodward. Zachery is married to Elizabeth Heiks.

Grandma Rhoda would be amazed to see her great-grandchildren, Fanny's descendants, traveling and living not only across the United States and Canada, but also in Antarctica, Belgium, China, the Congo, Germany, Haiti, Japan, South Korea, Tanzania and Tunisia. They are making their contributions in a global, technical world, much different from the smaller world Rhoda lived in.

Rhoda had only a third-grade formal education and Fanny a grade-school education. The progression of education in the family now ranges from high school to college to M.D. to Ph.D. Careers include architect, artist, biologist, builder, carpenter, computer programmer, designer, engineer, electrician, environmentalist, homemaker, librarian, medical doctor, nurse, photographer, radiologist, store manager, stage manager, teacher and welder.

As our heritage taught us, daily life is the place where faith happens. "Faith" was the word most used when our pioneer family talked about their families—"Faith is the substance of things hoped for, the evidence of things not seen" (Hebrews 11:1).

Emily Dickinson wrote, "This world is not conclusion; a sequel stands beyond."

works cited

Cather, Willa. *Shadow on the Rock*. Boston: Houghton Mifflin, 1938. Print.

Dickinson, Emily. "This world is not conclusion." *Complete Poems*. 1924. *Great Books Online*. 5 Jan. 2011 http://www.bartleby.com/113/4083.html

Eash, Sanford. "Just Abe and Fanny." Purpose 4 Feb. 1979: page 41. Print.

Familien Kalender: *Family Almanac*. Elkhart: Mennonitifdren Derlagshandlung, 1908. Print.

Gesang Buch: Geistreiche Lieder und Psalmen. Lancaster: Johann Bär and Sons, 1871. Print.

Holy Bible: The King James Version. Oxford: Oxford UP, 1963. Print.

Keillor, Garrison. Notable Quotes. 9 Jan. 2011 http://www.notable-quotes.com/k/keillor_garrison.html

Longfellow, Henry Wadsworth. "The Village Blacksmith." Bartleby. 5 Jan. 2011 http://www.bartleby.com/102/59.html

Luthy, David. "The Amish in Gosper County, Nebraska." *Yesterdays and Years* Aug. 1979: pages 19-21.

McDonald, Banks. Postcards to Rhoda Yoder, 1910-12. [These original handwritten postcards are in the possession of Twila Schrock of North Newton, KS.]

Miller, Brandon. "For My Friend" *Wind Word* Spring/Summer 2008: page 2. Print.

Stevenson, Robert Louis. *Across the Plains*. New York City: Charles Scribner's Sons, 1919.

Stoll, Fanny Mae Yoder. Personal journal, 15 February, 1972. [This original handwritten journal is in the possession of Twila Schrock of North Newton, KS.]

Stoll, Abraham Jonas. Personal journal, 15 February, 1972. [This original handwritten journal is in the possession of Twila Schrock of North Newton, KS.]

Yoder, Rhoda Ann Kauffman. Letters to Fanny Mae Stoll, 17 September, 1944. [These original handwritten letters are in the possession of Twila Schrock of North Newton, KS.]

Ward, May Williams. <u>Seesaw</u>. Atlanta: Bozart Press, 1929. Print.

photographs

[All family photographs are in the possession of Twila Schrock of North Newton, KS.]

about the author

Twila Schrock is a graduate of Moorhead State University with a B.A. in Education and Library Science. She taught as a librarian in Fargo Public Schools for 22 years. She and her husband are parents of four children and grandparents of eleven. She is retired and lives in North Newton, Kansas.

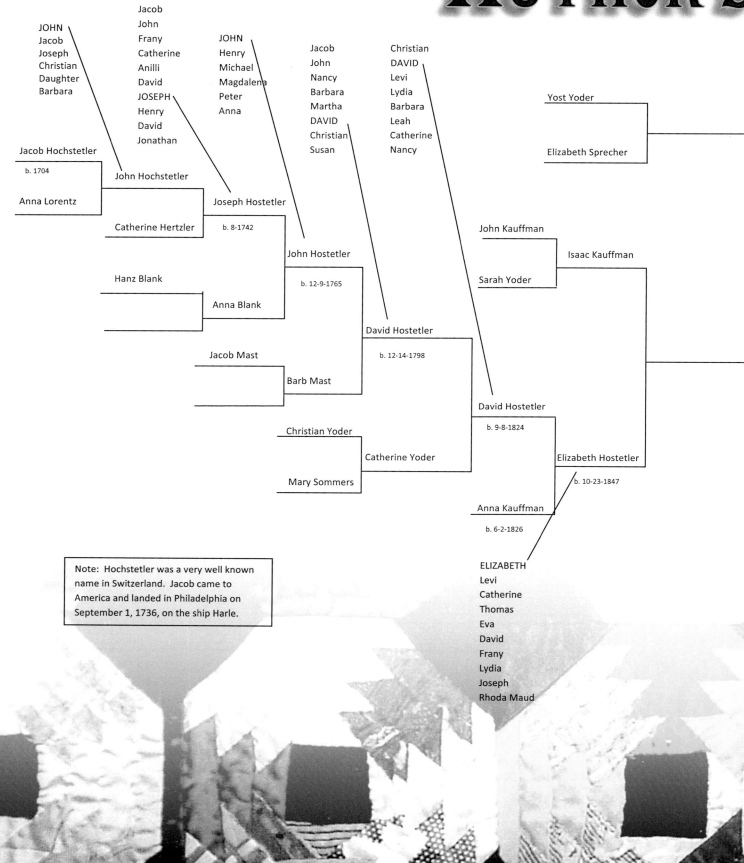

JOHN
Jacob
Joseph
Christian
Daughter
Barbara

Jacob
John
Frany
Catherine
Anilli
David
JOSEPH
Henry
David
Jonathan

JOHN
Henry
Michael
Magdalena
Peter
Anna

Jacob
John
Nancy
Barbara
Martha
DAVID
Christian
Susan

Christian
DAVID
Levi
Lydia
Barbara
Leah
Catherine
Nancy

Jacob Hochstetler
b. 1704

Anna Lorentz

John Hochstetler

Catherine Hertzler

Joseph Hostetler
b. 8-1742

Hanz Blank

Anna Blank

John Hostetler
b. 12-9-1765

Jacob Mast

Barb Mast

David Hostetler
b. 12-14-1798

Christian Yoder

Catherine Yoder

Mary Sommers

David Hostetler
b. 9-8-1824

Anna Kauffman
b. 6-2-1826

Elizabeth Hostetler
b. 10-23-1847

Yost Yoder

Elizabeth Sprecher

John Kauffman

Sarah Yoder

Isaac Kauffman

ELIZABETH
Levi
Catherine
Thomas
Eva
David
Frany
Lydia
Joseph
Rhoda Maud

Note: Hochstetler was a very well known name in Switzerland. Jacob came to America and landed in Philadelphia on September 1, 1736, on the ship Harle.